Intuitive Powe

Unlimited Life

LIMITING BELIEFS AND

BELIEF BUSTING POWER TRUTHS

Deborah Hill

Your Intuitive Life
Malaya Creations Publishing
Atlanta, Georgia

Copy Editor: Art Halperin
Illustrations: Rich Draper
Cover and Book Design/Layout: Deborah Hill, Online Creative, Inc.

Library of Congress Control Number: 2008904413
ISBN: 978-0-9817429-0-8

Published by: Malaya Creations
www.YourIntuitiveLife.com

Printed in the United States on acid free paper.
Distributed by Malaya Creations and New Leaf Distributing Company

For information:
Malaya Creations
5269 Glenridge Drive, Atlanta, Georgia 30342-1354. USA
www.YourIntuitiveLife.com

877-462-5292

Table of Contents

This book is dedicated to those who have supported me –
to my husband, parents, friends and especially to my clients who
have listened and flew. I have learned so much from you.

I'd also like to thank the friends and family who assisted with this book,
giving suggestions, edits and stories. My editor Art Halperin,
and my illustrator Rich Draper helped mold this book into
what it is today. To you all I give my undying gratitude.

My life has played out like a long, complex journey, full of promise, resistance, drive and perseverance. One of the things I've learned on my voyage is that we choose our beliefs, and these beliefs work best if they reflect who we truly are, what we want and what we honestly know. There is more to life than the mind – more to us. So much more. And it's all REAL. You may not believe me at first. So just read on, try out some of these concepts and then see for yourself. You'll discover your own truth. Knowledge from experience reaches far beyond belief and it's that magic that will set you free.

Introduction

Do you think of yourself as a unique powerhouse of dynamic energy, capable of creating a perfect life for yourself? You really are such a person. Do you know this? You have a wealth of abilities and talents that are just waiting to be unleashed, catapulting you into productive action. You're an amazing, talented individual – able to build, create, expand, enjoy, triumph, fly... but you may often feel stressed, frustrated and overwhelmed.

Walt Disney once said, "If you can dream it, you can do it." If that's true, why aren't you the master of your universe, leaping tall obstacles in a single bound? How did this dynamic powerhouse that we call "you" get hung up in pursuit of your dreams? It could be that you are simply standing in your own way. YOU may be your biggest obstacle. How? Your beliefs may be blocking you from being and doing all you can.

This book is about recognizing how your beliefs define who you are and what you can accomplish. You'll learn how to target these beliefs within you and replace them. I'll give you some examples of 'limiting beliefs' that many of us hold, and offer some powerful, belief busting truths to replace them with, so that you can be on your way to creating your dream life.

Introduction

In order to recognize your limiting beliefs, it's important to understand what you are and how life responds to you. Einstein revealed to us that everything is energy moving at different rates, including human bodies. Matter is merely energy moving slow enough to be detected by the five human senses: Seeing, hearing, tasting, feeling, and smelling. Our thoughts are energetic signals that pulsate through our brains, sending waves of energy through and around us. Our beliefs are repetitive, energetic thought patterns. Think of them as programmed vibrations within the brain. These belief "thought patterns" significantly influence our lives.

What we think and what we believe is reflected in the energy inside and surrounding us. Our thought and belief energy is projected from us like a radio tower projects radio waves. These energetic projections tell the universe and the people in it what's happening in our world. All of the other radio towers around us pick up this signal that we are broadcasting, and they respond accordingly. Everything in the universe will respond in-kind to this belief frequency. If we believe we're a failure, we broadcast this to the world and the world responds in kind. Likewise, if we believe we are well respected and successful we project it and it's mirrored back to us. Others tune in to our frequency and respond to it in much the same way they respond to what we physically say and do.

Introduction

What we think and believe helps to steer us through life and is mirrored back at us. An ancient principle called *The Law of Attraction* defines how we create and manifest in life. It says basically that all we have to do is ask for something, believe it will come to us, and it will. My experience has shown me that there are five steps involved in getting what you want for yourself:

1. Create a strong desire within you.

2. Clearly define what you want.

3. Remove all of your resistance to having it.

4. Ask for it.

5. Allow it to come to you.

You'll find that it is a simple technique and it works magically.

Esther Hicks describes The Law of Attraction as, "That which is like unto itself is drawn. Which means vibrations are always balanced. So as you experience the contrast which inspires the new idea within you, this new idea – this desire – whether it is strong, or soft, is summoning unto itself proportionately. And as it summons, it is always answered."

Each of us is composed of energy and the energy that defines us is constantly vibrating. These vibrations change according to who we are, what we think, how we feel... and all that's happening within us at any given moment. According to *The Law of Attraction* you create your own reality through your vibrations by summoning what you want.

Wait, can that be right? Just ask for what you want and you get it? Nothing in life is that simple! If it were, everybody would be getting everything they wanted. Why aren't you living in a beautiful beach house with billions of dollars in your pocket? Or, taking that world vacation you've always dreamed about? Why haven't you found that perfect relationship? You want it. You define it. You ask for it. So where is it? Wouldn't you know, there's a catch: Your vibration may be moving in opposition to your desires. Your thinking, or your beliefs may not support your wants and needs. In order to be that magnet that attracts what you want, your beliefs must support your needs, dreams and desires. What do you believe? It's important to pay attention to this if you want to create your perfect life.

Introduction

For years I held a belief that people didn't like me. I developed this belief early in life, or perhaps it was just part of my character. Maybe, someone close to me told me I was unlikable and I believed it. Or, I may have deduced it by taking other people's reactions personally. Hey, maybe I really was unlikable. Whatever the reason, I felt separate from everyone else and unaccepted.

Looking back, I now realize that I was being extremely intuitive. I was seeing, hearing and feeling things that others didn't. I was very sensitive to other people's energy. So, I took their responses to me, and feelings about me personally. In other words, I believed that I was the epicenter of everyone else's opinions and beliefs about me. If a friend became angry, my perception was that he didn't like me and therefore something was wrong with me. If a stranger called me a name I immediately owned it and I regretted being that way. Not a very effective way of dealing with life, but it's the way it was at the time.

You've probably noticed that when people get angry they often blame others for their anger. People call each other names and criticize each other regularly. Why did I take responsibility for their actions? Chalk it up to misdirected thought. Left unchecked, these miss-thoughts can accumulate into a programmed pile called a "belief." I honestly believed that when people were angry with me and criticized me, I was to blame, and therefore something was wrong with me. I tried to make people happy and like me. I attempted to heal everyone of their pain and suffering so they wouldn't be mad at me or criticize me. This strategy was about as effective as trying to move Mt. Rainier one bucket of dirt at a time.

I also tried to change me to suit everyone else. As you might expect, that didn't work out too well either. I failed at overcoming all of the anger and criticism in the world. I couldn't change myself enough to prevent it, so I believed there was something wrong with me. My beliefs told me that I did not fit in and I wasn't likeable. A pretty sorry state, but I'm not throwing a pity party here.

My own situation is a prime example of how right, or wrong, a belief system is developed and perpetuated. I created my own truth – that others didn't like me and I just didn't belong. Because beliefs are a form of energy I projected this belief out into the world. When

someone met me they may have subcons

and gone along with my projection. The my

my perception of it). I kept seeing it, kept believi

the pattern continued.

showe

cam

to

When General Eisenhower ran for President, many people showed their support by wearing "I LIKE IKE" buttons throughout the campaign. As a child, I always felt just the opposite. One day a coach told me that I was wearing a "You Do Not Like Me" belief like a sign in my energetic field. This "sign" was being picked up by others before I even spoke. No matter what I said or did, the sign was getting in the way. She suggested that I ditch it. This seemed like a very good idea. Although I envisioned it would require years of psychological counseling, reprogramming, meditations and alternative healing.

It then occurred to me that I'd already spent years in self-treatment. I decided I wanted immediate results. I wasn't willing to play the "you don't like me" game anymore. If I had a "sign" there was just one thing to do. Once and for all change it. In the words made famous by Nike, "Just Do it." Without regard for why I had been carrying the sign, or whether it was a justified belief, I ditched my "sign" and replaced it with another. Here's how I did it: I sat quietly alone and visualized myself being surrounded by my aura of energy. I imagined a sign in my aura that said "You don't like me." I then took this sign and trashed it.

I blew it to smithereens. Then I brought out one that said, "I'm a great person, you're going to like me." I even added a little neon and flashing lights for emphasis.

Try as I might, that pesky old sign kept reappearing. I exploded it from my energetic field with virtual missiles. I stomped it flat. I replaced it with my new sign over and over again. Whenever I met someone new, or entered a room full of people, I projected that I was wearing the new sign that said, "I'm a great person and you're going to like me." I did my best to believe in the power of the sign. I had to pull out all of my stubborn resignation and force this belief on myself. An inner "self-pity" voice tried its best to convince me that it wasn't true. I determinedly ignored her. When people got mad at me I wanted to haul out the old sign again, but I didn't. I trusted my new instinct and stuck with it.

Boy, did that new sign ever do the trick! People started smiling at me. They invited me to go places. They told me how much they liked me. Most importantly, I liked me and I was happy. I believed I was likeable and it felt GOOD! The belief was working for me. I saw how I fit in and my dream life began to unfold.

Your beliefs may be limiting your own success and happiness in much the same way. One indication is the patterns occurring in your life. Notice when you're playing out one of these patterns. You can use it to pinpoint a belief that may be hanging you up. Start by asking yourself, "What do I

feel right now?" You may hear something like, "I feel hurt and left out." Go along with this. Empathize with that voice. Have compassion for yourself. Justified or not, a part of you feels this way.

Be your own best friend and ask the voice to continue. Let your feelings express themselves not just in words, but also in thoughts. These thoughts are the patterns that you carry within you. They comprise and perpetuate your belief. You may hear your inner voice saying things that may or may not sound true at the objective level. For example it may say, "I feel stupid and silly." Be a good listener and don't negate these feelings. Hear yourself out. Then open your heart to you and have compassion for the part of you that thinks and feels this way.

Realize that true or not, the negative thoughts that you're having aren't working for you. Tell yourself: "This thought is perpetuating the unwanted state of affairs in my life. By not challenging it, I will cause the pattern to reoccur." Try experimenting with a new, more positive thought. Simply swap the old "sign" inside your head for a new one. You can write an affirmation that turns the belief around to something that's positive, such as: "I'm smart, capable and totally adept at making the correct decisions for my life."

If your limiting belief is saying you'll never find that dream relationship you desire, create an affirmation instead: "The love of my life is at my doorstep." If you think your dreams are impossible to accomplish, affirm "I am the master at creating my life and can do this one step at a time."

Next, use the following meditation to adopt the new concept: Sit quietly and breathe deeply. Focus from a place within the center of your head. Pull out your internal markers (or art supplies) and create a visual sign to put up within your energetic field. Visualize taking down the old sign and replacing it with the new one.

Introduction

To reinforce your new belief sign, write the affirmation on a note and post it in a conspicuous place that can't be ignored. You may feel hesitant at first. You may hear a voice within you that doesn't accept the new belief. Your old thinking probably wore a groove in your brain and you'll need to rewire, or reprogram your thinking. Convince yourself to try out this new thought and reject your old belief thoughts. Act as if the new belief is true. Consciously project this new thought pattern. You may need to repeat the meditation several times, or visualize the new truth whenever you feel stress or resistance within you. If you engage in this exercise you'll notice that your life will magically change. Soon the new belief will become a patterned projection and you will be living the dream life you desire.

We each have our own unique hang-ups or beliefs that we can change. We also share a number of common limiting beliefs. Throughout this book I will be addressing a variety of common, limiting beliefs that may be keeping you from creating the life you desire; and truths that you can replace these beliefs with. These beliefs are not ranked in order of importance. Each one is capable of making your life miserable in its own way. It's very possible that you are harboring some very special limiting beliefs of your own. The examples in this book may provide helpful clues on how to spot limiting beliefs within you. You'll discover how they work and how to change them. Armed with this new awareness, you'll soon be able to replace them with your own powerful truths.

Limiting Belief 1

It's too much for me. I just can't do it.

As a child I loved the story, <u>The Little Engine That Could</u>. The engine in the story kept saying, "I think I can. I think I can. I think I can," as it tried to pull the heavy train up the mountain. And the belief that it could was all the power that the little engine needed to accomplish its mission. The story is inspiring and the message is true. Henry Ford said it well: "If you think you can do a thing or think you can't do a thing, you're right." I discovered an ancillary truth that can give you and extra shove up that mountain: If you're asked to do something you can do it.

You may be given a task that you feel is too difficult, too time consuming, or too tiring. It's easy to come up with a variety of excuses for why you can't do it. There are powerful truths to counter countless excuses like these. I've tried this replacement belief out more times than I can count and it's worked every time: If someone asks you to do something (and they aren't being malicious or trying to be funny) you can do it. You don't have to do it, but if the task is presented to you, you're capable. Energetically it won't come up for you if you don't have what it takes to do it.

I discovered this truth when I was asked to coach at a conference in Colorado. I was told that I would be conducting fifteen minute consecutive coaching sessions with few breaks, for three days straight. At first, the task seemed impossible to me. I like to help people discover the core issue that's blocking them, understand and work through it. But how could I possibly coach one person for fifteen minutes, then move on to the next person? How could I continue to do this for three days? I projected a task that would be not only impossible to complete, but also totally exhausting.

I knew that if I attended the conference and led the sessions, I'd potentially help a lot of people. It would be a rewarding experience, and I wanted to give it a try. But, I had this doubt in my mind. I believed it was impossible. So, rather than admitting defeat and turning down the offer, I decided to reprogram my thinking based on this belief: "I'm capable of doing something if someone asks me to it. I don't have to do what is requested. I can say 'no.' It's totally up to me. However, I am capable of doing the task well if it's presented to me."

It became clear to me that we are presented with physical challenges and obstacles that match our energy. We project and life responds. If this is true, how can something that is totally foreign to us come our way? There has to be a place that is magnetically drawing this energy to us. If we are presented with an opportunity or a task, we are energetically drawing this task to us. We are therefore ready for it.

With my new belief in place, I agreed to conduct the three days of coaching sessions. Whenever I sensed my mind voicing a fear or doubt I told myself, "If it's asked of you, you're able to do it." Because the situation required it, I quickly found ways of identifying the core issues confronting each client. As the days passed, I was amazed at how quickly I communicated what the person needed to hear.

I knew the conference would be stressful, so I made self-care a priority. Professional healers were available and I signed up for massages and healing sessions whenever I had free time. Besides lots of pampering, I got the extra bonus of learning new techniques and meeting some extraordinary people.

Instead of collapsing in bed and ordering room service in the evenings, I made dinner reservations at a fine restaurant nearby. I bought bath salts and I made soaking in a rejuvenating bath a luxury that I looked forward to every night after dinner. The preparations and the new belief I had installed in my mind paid off handsomely. I conducted sixty-four coaching sessions over the span of three days. I took satisfaction in seeing most of the people that I coached experience a meaningful transformation in a very short time. It was amazing! I didn't know I was capable of accomplishing such a feat. Obviously, I was destined to take this next step and I went for it. Now, I travel to Colorado almost every year for a three-day weekend and help forty to sixty people work through issues in their lives. Instead of dreading the experience I look forward to it and I love it.

Next time you face a situation that seems too difficult for you, think of it this way: If you're asked to do something, the person asking you believes that you're capable of doing it. Why not adopt the same belief in your own mind? If you're given a task that you don't think you're ready for, say to yourself, "Everything is energetically connected. The energy in front of me is on my path because it's connected to my energy. I can do this." The truth is that this project, or task, or situation is on your path, because you're already a part of it. You're capable of accomplishing it because you're one with it.

Power Truth 1

If I'm asked to do something, I'm capable of doing it.

Unlimited Life

Limiting Belief 2

I don't have enough time.

It's happened to most of us. We look at a lengthy to-do list, or the impossible pile of work waiting on our desk and we can't imagine how we will get it all done. We picture a time line, then we try to fit the projects into it like pieces of a puzzle. But, the pieces don't fit.

This belief, that there isn't enough time, is based on the assumption that time is linear. It isn't. The truth is that our minds function in a material, three-dimensional world. The rational mind responds to what it sees, hears and the body feels. It only picks up signals from these material aspects of three-dimensional life.

The mind is also programmed to think linearly. It cannot truly understand how time works because time is not linear. If it were, time would only operate in two-dimensions. Our physical bodies function in three dimensions. But as Albert Einstein noted, time is the fourth dimension. Therefore time is not constrained by three physical dimensions. It is happening simultaneously and can go in many directions. The truth is, in this fourth dimension time is unlimited. The misbelief that there isn't enough time comes from a three-dimensional view of things. It takes a more profound, non-linear, thinking to understand this concept. The rational mind sees life with fourth dimensional blinders on. Trying to understand the fourth dimension with a rational mind is like trying to turn a straight line into a cube. It can't be done.

Fortunately, you don't have to understand the fourth dimension to make this belief work. It will work if you just believe it. The new truth regarding time is simply that time is unlimited. Try this belief on. Imagine for a while that time is plentiful. Let go of the belief – the worry – that you don't have enough of it to accomplish tasks, or to meet your goals.

Pretend that time is like an ocean that goes in all directions. Or, visualize a bubble floating through the air. You're the bubble and the air is time. Or, forget about visualizing and simply let go of the belief that you don't have enough time. Instead, adopt the belief that time is unlimited. Next, just do whatever task is in front of you at the moment. Take one step at a time and don't waste your energy trying to figure out how you'll get it all done.

Energy is a valuable commodity. Why waste it on unproductive activities like worrying that we may not have enough time? We want to use our energy to accomplish what it is we need and want to do. Instead of worrying about time (or anything) we can use it to have a good time. When the limiting belief pops up that says we don't have enough time, we can replace it with the belief that says time is unlimited. Change the thought. Just know that everything will get done in time and trust me, it will. Time and space will magically adjust to you.

I've owned my own graphic design business for nineteen years. And, like many businesses, the work comes in spurts. There are times when no work is coming in. Then a flood of work appears. I used to stress out about the ever-changing workload. When the floodgates opened I'd lose sleep worrying about how I could possibly complete all of the work on time. I'd work nights and weekends, even to the point of illness. During the slow times I wondered if I'd survive, and this kept me up at night.

One year I had a particularly slow summer. A worried voice within me pondered the possibility that my career could be over. I had nothing to do and no projects on the horizon. Then suddenly my phone began to ring. Several clients called to say they were sending me work that had to be completed on an accelerated schedule. They were counting on me. Just like that I was in demand.

Then the irony struck me: If I added up all the hours of work facing me, I'd have felt this task was impossible to accomplish. Especially if I also expected to eat, exercise, sleep, have friends and enjoy time with my husband – all of the other aspects of life that are important to me. But, I didn't add up the hours. I decided that I'd take on a new belief: Time is unlimited and I will have enough of it to accomplish everything asked of me and complete the task on time. I kept saying, "Yes," when additional work was presented to me and I just did what was on my desk that day.

Two very interesting things happened. First, when I stopped

worrying I was able to accomplish a great deal more. I worked efficiently and got things done in much less time. Second, as it turned out, not all of my clients actually got their projects to me when they said they would. So the impossible scenario shifted so that each project presented itself exactly when I had the time for it.

I used this understanding of how time works when I was on a retreat with some friends in Hawaii. Our group took a side trip to a very remote cave to participate in a powerful meditation. The experience was rewarding, but it ran longer than we anticipated. We were concerned that we hadn't left ourselves enough time to get back to our hotel for our next activity. The return trip would take an hour and a half. But our next session would be starting in an hour and fifteen minutes. I made a decision and an intent that we would arrive in one hour and fifteen minutes. I didn't speed. There were no traffic lights to consider. I did nothing to hurry our ride home. But, I firmly believed that we would get there in the allotted time. And we did. The leader of the retreat was amazed. She'd been to the cave hundreds of times and it always took her an hour and a half to return. It seemed like magic to her when we arrived so quickly. I knew it wasn't magic. Time only seems magical when you view it in a three-dimensional world.

My experience of my friend's son, Whit also exemplifies this concept of time:

"Whit (a busy CPA) was traveling along the interstate on his way to a business appointment when he saw the tire blow out on a car ahead of him. The woman driving it pulled the car off to the service shoulder without incident.

As he drove past her disabled vehicle, Whit told himself he'd be late meeting with his client if he stopped to help her.

By the time he reached the next exit he had a change of heart. He turned off, crossed over and back tracked to where he could come up behind the stranded vehicle. "Bless you, bless you," the woman said. "I saw you go by and prayed you'd come back." She was on her way to a job interview and was heartsick over the possibility of missing, or being late for it.

To Whit's surprise, despite the detour he actually arrived at his client's office on time, though a little on the sweaty side."

The truth is we have as much time as we need. Time is flexible and unlimited. It bends with our belief about how it works. If we believe it's linear and limited, it will seem that way. If we believe we have enough time, we will.

Time may be a tough concept, but here's a suggestion for using this truth: When you feel yourself becoming stressed about not having enough time, verbalize to yourself that time is unlimited and you have as much as you need. Let go of your resistance to the new concept. Then focus only on what is happening in the present. Don't look ahead, as this will create worry. Pull your focus back to the task at hand and give it your full attention. You can treat this as an experiment, saying "I know this seems crazy, but let's pretend that I have enough time." Then see what happens. Say to yourself, "If I don't accomplish this task, I'll worry about it later." Once you practice this technique you'll see that you're in control, and you'll stop feeling pressured by time.

Power Truth 2

Time is unlimited. I have as much time as I need.

Limiting Belief 3

A specific task always takes the
same amount of time to accomplish.

A task doesn't always have to take the same amount of time every time you perform it. Many of us limit ourselves by believing that a task has to take a specific amount of time, especially if we've done it before. We may think, "Washing and drying my hair takes twenty minutes no matter what." Or, "I need three days to put together a proposal." But, you may be able to get more done in a shorter period of time, and still get the same quality result.

My daughter was married on the opposite coast. If you've ever tried to plan a wedding from a considerable distance, you know how time and labor intensive the project can be. My businesses picked up at the very same time. My desk was flooded with incoming design projects, plus I was doing a lot of coaching and teaching. I felt completely overwhelmed. Getting everything done before the day my daughter walked down the aisle seemed impossible. My belief in having unlimited time was intact, but the project load kept growing.

I finally realized that I was limiting myself by assuming how much time each task would take. For example, I believed that it would take ten hours to design a brochure. So I allocated ten hours to designing it. But since I had other things vying for my time, I decided that I could design that same brochure in just five hours and it would be the best brochure that I'd ever designed – totally fulfilling my client's needs and exemplary in quality.

My mind didn't adapt to the new belief very well. It said, "You've been doing this for years and it's always taken you ten hours. How can you do a good job in less time? It's impossible."

I decided to ignore my mind's ranting. I acknowledged that on previous projects creative energy would pour into me at a certain rate. I decided to up the amperage of my creative generator. I adopted the belief that I could not only move, but also store more creative energy at the same time – a form of multi-tasking. Instead of streaming in slowly, I visualized the design for this brochure coming to me as a flood of creative thought, and exploding onto the page. I also visualized the brochure looking equal to, or better than any I'd designed in the past. I firmly believed that this would happen and it did. Fresh and innovative designs filled the pages, flowing from my heart to my hands and into the computer. It felt like a tidal wave of creativity washing over me. Not only did I have enough time to do a superior job, I had a lot of fun doing it.

Since I didn't waste time on extraneous thoughts, I was able to focus more clearly. I'd bid the job as a fixed price project. So by completing the assignment in half the time I effectively doubled my hourly rate. Not only was I more creative, I'd given myself a raise in the process! The wedding planning was equally productive and the event was a complete success.

The truth is, your belief greatly influences how much time you take to complete a task; and in reality it can take much less time than you think. Here's a suggestion for how you can accomplish more in less time than you thought possible. Notice when you first begin to think, "This project is going to take more time than I have." It shouldn't be difficult to notice this because you'll probably be fretting quite a bit about it. Step back from your emotions and breathe. Then objectively calculate how much time you believe you have to accomplish the task. Next, focus on your solar plexus, between your heart and naval, and imagine that the energy in that area is increasing. While opening that area, tell yourself, "I don't have six hours to do this. It will be done in three hours. I know it can be done because I only have three hours. I have complete faith in myself that I can accomplish this. I won't worry about it because worrying takes time. I will stay focused and believe it will happen and it will." Repeat this whenever the worry surfaces.

Power Truth 3

Projects will take as much time as I intend them to.

Unlimited Life

Limiting Belief 4

I can accurately visualize my future.

This concept's a bit tricky as we are taught from childhood to visualize and plan our future. We're told to dream big and follow these dreams. I'm not saying to stop dreaming and planning. In fact, I believe that we create our lives through our dreams, desires and plans. However, the truth is, life will never turn out exactly as you visualize it. You can't accurately predict how the future will look, or be played out because there are aspects of the future that you can't see right now.

If someone had told my Eastern European immigrant grand-mother in 1909 that as an adult she'd travel every winter from Michigan to Florida, she'd be astounded (for many reasons). For one thing, she could not imagine making such a trip on a regular basis because she didn't know that cars would be widely accessible, that freeways would be built; or the airplane would become a common mode of transportation. She could dream about having a life where she lived in Michigan and wintered in Miami. But, there would be no way she could visualize how this could happen.

We may hit a wall if we believe that we can accurately visualize the future. We may imagine this incredible picture of the life that we want to create and then think, "It seems impossible." We visualize how wonderful it could be then think to ourselves, "How will I ever be able to achieve that (be that, or have that)?" Or simply think, "That can never happen." Our dream or vision looks too big and unattainable from where we're standing in present time. It seems overwhelming and impossible. If you have ever been anxious about the future for any reason you have probably succumbed to this belief.

We can dream and plan, but we can't really envision what the future will hold because we aren't there yet. For example, I used to be deadly serious... seriously serious. I believed that amusement is one of the most valuable assets in living a happy life and I was in trouble. I tried for years to be amusing and I was failing. I knew I needed help and help showed up in the form of Jeff Justice. Jeff teaches seriously serious people like me to loosen up and be funny. He helps comedians and "the rest of us" to see the humor in life and project it. I signed up for his class, knowing I was going to be a tough case. He predicted that in just six weeks I would learn how to be funny and find amusement in life. I couldn't imagine it. I could dream about it and plan on it. But, I just couldn't see the future with a funny me in it.

On the first day Jeff told us that our class that we would be performing our own comedy routine in front of a full house at the Punchline Comedy Club in Atlanta for our graduation, AND we would be great on stage. That seemed absurd. Not only couldn't I imagine it, the idea of me standing up there trying to make others laugh was the scariest thing that I'd ever thought about. I would have been less anxious if you'd told me I was going to die in six weeks. I could not imagine being funny.

For the next six weeks I was a serious student of comedy. I would take the class, and step-by-step learn how to be funny. I wrote bad jokes. I would learn how to write good ones, and by the next round I would be a little funnier. I would have numerous sessions standing in front of the class telling jokes that fell through the floor. I'd rework my jokes countless times, learning by trial and error what it takes to be funny. More importantly, I would learn how to laugh at myself. That was one of the most powerful lessons I've ever learned. I could not envision how I'd progress day-by-day. I knew I would be different but there was no way I could imagine how. My inability to believe that I'd get applause at the Punchline was understandable. I couldn't accurately visualize it because I wasn't there yet.

We can dream about the future or worry about it. But these visualizations are never completely accurate because we haven't taken the steps needed to get there. Each step changes us and when we arrive we're a different person than the one that started.

The world changes, too. When the Wright brothers invented the first successful airplane, they knew in theory it was possible to fly. After all, birds did it. But they did not know how they could make it happen on their terms. Others thought the Wrights were insane because people flying in airplanes was unimaginable at the time. The brothers tried and failed many times before perfecting their invention – a design that was not predictable before. When they finally flew they were smarter than when they started. Still, even though they thought they would one day fly, they could never have dreamed what it would actually feel like to be soaring through the air on that particular machine.

When I was a young adult I tried to visualize what I would do with my life. I was studying to become a doctor at the time. If someone had told me I would become a graphic artist working on a computer and communicating with people all over the world via something called the internet, I'd have thought they were crazy. I didn't see myself as an artist, for one thing. The personal computer hadn't been invented yet, for another. Even if it had, I didn't think of myself as a decent typist. I couldn't imagine that a machine would be invented that would allow me to use my right brain and left brain (and a device called a mouse) to create art. It would have been a ludicrous concept for me at the time – maybe even frightening. However, in 1984 I bought the first Apple Macintosh® to write my Masters Thesis in Nursing.

I loved that Mac and I evolved as it did. My graphic design talents developed naturally and effortlessly when the time was right and the tools were available. I wasn't just an artist. I was a techno artist working on a computer – an artistic geek with a strong science background. There is no way I could have foreseen that development. I had changed and most importantly, the world had changed around me.

Have you ever considered moving to a new city... getting married... expanding your business... or changing careers? It may seem scary or wonderful to imagine new scenarios. They may seem overwhelming or impossible to create. But they're not. If you try to put yourself in the final phase of the dream you may feel overwhelmed because you and the world aren't there yet.

Winston Churchill said, "It is a mistake to try to look too far ahead. The chain of destiny can only be grasped one link at a time." Heed Churchill's advice and everything will take shape when you and life are ready for it. Remember, you can dream it, but can't visualize it completely because neither you nor life are evolved enough for you to be there yet. But don't let that stop you. Go ahead – dream, hope and plan away – and don't be frightened of the unknown.

Anticipation can be overrated. Living in the present we're able to do anything we plan to do. We're ready for today, and we're able to take on whatever is presented to us in the moment. We may anticipate or dread the future. But, we can never know what it will feel like and be like. Just taking one step at a time we can do just about anything. Just keep dreaming and stepping and soon you will be there. You'll be wiser and stronger and in a new place.

The truth is, you can accomplish more than you dream of if you stay focused in present time and just do what's in front of you. If you feel yourself becoming overwhelmed by something you feel you need to accomplish do this: Stop looking into the future. Tell yourself that the future is created by a series of "nows" that occur one "now" at a time. You can address the problem or the opportunity that's directly in front of you. Focus on that and only that. Tomorrow you'll tackle what comes up for you then. One day at time – one moment at a time – you can handle whatever comes your way. Practice that and in no time you'll be living your dream.

Power Truth 4

I can create anything I dream, one step at a time.

Limiting Belief 5

We must dwell on our past mistakes so we don't repeat them.

At first glance this limiting belief seems very logical and realistic. We learn from early childhood that the past repeats itself, and we are lead to believe: As before so after. Teachers reveal that certain blunders have been repeated throughout history. Great leaders have extolled us to recognize our past mistakes so we won't repeat them. However the belief that the past repeats itself is somewhat misleading. Actions may reoccur, but the circumstances that bring them about are never exactly the same. The past is never exactly the same when it is projected into the present or the future. Life changes. The world changes. Society changes. You change.

We all look back and see the past differently. Our view of the past is probably not even accurate. In a recent "Weekend America" issue, Suzie Lechtenberg transcribed her interview with Larry Lehmer. Larry recalled, "When I interviewed Waylon Jennings for the book, he kind of carried some guilt with him for a long time, because he had given up his seat to the Big Bopper. There were so many people that claimed that they'd given up that seat on the plane, which was a four seater. Obviously not everyone could have fit on it. He says that if everyone that says they were supposed to be on that plane, was on that plane, they'd of needed a 747."

We often try to remember the past so that we don't repeat our mistakes. Albert Einstein said, "Insanity is merely doing the same thing over and over again and expecting different results." Yes, that would be crazy. But, few people actually do that.

Have you ever made a mistake that reminded you of one that you had made before? If you really think about it, there are elements that made the experience significantly different the second time around. If you were able to accurately remember how you acted before, would you really act differently in the present? Maybe not. Though experiences seem the same, we learn something new each time because the situation is always slightly different. We change and react differently based upon this new knowledge.

Trying to fit past experience into the present is like trying to wear a suit you wore twenty years ago. Even if you can still fit into it it's out of style. The same goes for relationships. You know that you can never relive your first kiss. Each kiss is unique to the exact moment and to the person you're with. You may also see many beautiful sunsets, but each one will be special and memorable in its own way – depending upon the location, the circumstances involved and the person you're sharing it with.

One experience doesn't foretell the infinite variety and depth of those that follow. Daffodils bloom every spring, but their patterns and flowers are never quite the same. No two snowflakes are exactly alike. Mistakes and negative experiences may appear to repeat themselves. But, in truth each experience is unique.

When we dwell on and fear repeating our past mistakes we live partially in the past – a past that we may not even remember correctly. We don't clearly see what's actually happening around us. Remembering previous mistakes may contribute to our feelings of Déjà vu, because we project our fear of the past onto the present. We experience something that seems familiar; and then we anticipate the exact same outcome as before. We expect to live through replays of the same events over and over. But in reality, we just see them fitting the same template and in doing so we shape our present to be more like the past. If we dwell on the past we live out the same memories, like having a bad dream over and over.

It's said that a truly intelligent person doesn't make the same mistake twice. We assume that we need to remember past mistakes so that we don't repeat them. But what if we just learn the lesson and let go of the memory of the scenario that spawned it? What if we automatically learned from each mistake and that lesson became a part of us. Being present we're able to make use of valuable lessons in a way that living in the past doesn't. If we pay attention to what's happening now and trust our inner knowing, we'll make the right decisions in present time. The times and the environment will change and we will change. A similar experience, or emotion, or challenge may come up, but we'll react to it differently each time, because we are different if we trust our knowing.

Releasing the past frees us to create a brighter future. This may be a scary proposition to us if we believe that our memory of past situations is what prevents us from repeating them. If such were the case, a person with Alzheimer's Disease would reach out and touch a flame. Toddlers with no memory of their actions as an infant would continue the same behavior as when they were babies. The truth is that we learn from making mistakes. In spirit that is how we essentially grow. The lesson is not only learned, but also retained, ready to be recalled whenever we need it. All we have to do is pay attention to our inner voice – that soft, yet strong alert system that we sometimes call our "conscience." When we tap this inner knowing, or gut feeling, we avoid making similar mistakes. We are free to trust our instincts and most importantly stay focused on the present. In doing so, our knowledge base is available to us, instead of our fears of the past.

Henry Ford said, "History is more or less bunk." The best place to put the past is behind you. Trust yourself to have learned your lesson. Then be strong enough to follow your own inner guidance. You'll still make mistakes because that is how we learn. But, you'll never make the same mistake in the same way. Moments are like snowflakes. Each one is different. You'll create new experiences through new understanding gained from past experiences (and mistakes).

By the same token, don't fear the past. If you do, you'll only project it into the present. Trust yourself to handle life as it comes. You'll find that each experience is new and unique, offering a fuller understanding of the present.

The truth is, dwelling on the past contributes to you reliving it. You are new each day – each moment. You have learned your lessons and are capable of creating a bright new future.

If you find yourself fretting about, or regretting your past – or even gloating about your accomplishments – pull yourself back to the present. The past isn't reality any longer. It doesn't exist in this moment. You don't even see it accurately. Instead, focus on what is happening now and deal with that. Take a deep breath. Look around you. Be present. Make a decision to use your energy to create now, and not to watch old re-runs of your past life.

Power Truth 5

When Life changes, I change. I learn and move forward.

Unlimited Life

Limiting Belief 6

I can understand others and why they behave the way they do.

People have probably been trying to figure each other out since the human race came into existence. You may have begun the process at an early age with questions like, "How can I get Mom to give me candy?" Or, "How can I stay up past my bed time and not get in trouble?" Most of us ask ourselves questions on a daily basis. Questions like: "Why did he do that?" Or, "What can I say to make her understand?" Or, "How can I get to know him better?" Thousands of books have been written giving guidelines and advice on the subject of understanding others. People have developed personality evaluation systems and maps ranging from astrology to ink blots and body language. These diverse analytical techniques give us insight into human traits and patterns. Through them we learn to recognize generalized traits in others and develop compassion, empathy and new ways to communicate. Yet try as we may, we are never able to truly experience what it's like to be someone else. Therefore, we can never truly understand another person completely.

We may be similar in many ways. We may have compassion and see "eye-to-eye," but we can never truly walk in another person's shoes. Each person has an essential essence that has its own unique character and vibration. We can see other people's vibrations and feel them. But, we can't be them.

What does this mean to you? You can never completely figure out why someone is doing something that affects you. You'll never fully know why the guy in front of you cut across three lanes of traffic to turn right from the left hand lane. You'll never understand why the woman in the next booth is wearing a purple checked scarf with a green plaid blouse and orange skirt. I know I'll never understand how people can swim in our health club's outdoor pool when it's 34 degrees outside (heated or not!). It's beyond my comprehension. Yet, it's obviously the right thing for them to be doing or they wouldn't be there.

Imagine all the time and energy it would save if we stopped assuming that we knew what was best for each other. We wouldn't judge others, because we'd know that we don't truly understand their motivation.

I had a conversation with a friend while on vacation. Walking through a ski lodge she was telling me about a situation at her place of work. After I listened and commented, I thought the conversation was finished. I then began paying attention to an irritation caused by my new ski boots. I made an expression that my friend interpreted as disapproval of her. She questioned me about it and I was surprised. My friend assumed that my expression was directed at her. It wasn't. I'm glad she brought it up so I could explain my position. If gone unchecked, her assumption could have lead to resentment and damage to our relationship.

When we accept that we don't truly know another we can learn to live with respect and appreciation of each other. Maybe we'll try harder to communicate clearly, knowing that each person hears and interprets things differently. We may not be as quick to react to something someone says or does if we're aware that we don't truly understand why they are saying or doing it.

My friend Joe recounted a story of an experience early in his career: "I'll never forget a conversation I had with a client. I called to inquire about a project that was supposed to be coming up and he sounded irritated. This disturbed me because I thought I'd said or done something to upset him. He heard my concern and said, 'You may not be responsible for what I'm feeling. A lot goes on in my day that you don't know about. Maybe I had a fight with my wife. I might feel a flu coming on.' I learned that the way a person reacts to you has nothing to do with you." If we all realized the truth of this statement we may be more ourselves, not taking things personally or trying to change for another.

If we stop assuming that we understand others, life becomes more interesting as each person presents a unique opportunity to see a different part of life. While we may understand certain patterns in people, we will never truly "get" them until we treat every interaction with an open mind, and even curiosity. Our communications will stay new and fresher. If we don't assume that we know why another person said something, or acted in a certain way, we avoid arguments and resentments. Life will be less stressful because we don't feel responsible for other people's actions.

Power Truth 6

You can see eye-to-eye, but you can't walk in another's shoes.

Limiting Belief 7

I can fix someone else or another's problems.

Even if it were possible to change, or fix someone else, consider why you'd want to attempt it in the first place. Are you looking for personal rewards from this? Your immediate response may be, "Absolutely not. How could you even think of me that way?" But, look again. Many people try to fix another person because the other person irritates them. It's tough being around people who are hurting themselves, or messing up their life in some way. It sometimes seems easier to fix a person (or try to) than to live with him while he fixes himself.

Living with people we love while they are working through an "issue" is seriously difficult for most people. In fact, it is one of the toughest things we'll ever do. Birthing a baby is taxing, but it only lasts for a few hours. Coexisting with someone working through an issue can mean having to deal with it for years. It's even more difficult when we think we have the cure or the answer. We just want it to be over t to see the other person happy and "right" according to

...s.

...this very problem with my daughter. Or, more accurately, she had it with me. When she was younger she was trying desperately to find her own way in life. This is very appropriate for a teenager or young adult. (Or even older adults). But, I hated to see her struggling. I didn't want to see her fail in life. So, I made suggestions. A lot of suggestions. I even nagged her about a few of them. A lot. Needless to say, we were both miserable.

"Why won't you listen to me? You never listen to me," I pleaded. "You'd make a terrific graphic artist... a teacher... or whatever." Sometimes she did listen, but my vision of how she should live her life never matched her own. Finally, I got that she was very capable of finding her own way. So I stopped preaching to her and began supporting her. Not surprisingly she eventually found her career and is very happy with it.

Some people try to fix others because they like being appreciated. Helping others is a way to boost their low self-esteem. This is a sad situation because the fixer's self-esteem is based on someone else's

approval. If the person they're "fixing" isn't fixed, or doesn't apprec͜ɪ
ate what they're doing they're in trouble with their self. That's not a
pleasant place to be.

Instead, true self-esteem comes from love of self. Otherwise,
we're on shaky ground. If we need to get approval from another person we're on their terms and their territory – neither of which has anything to do with us. We have no control of how someone else is going
to respond to us or to our advice. (see Power Truth 6.)

Why is it impossible to fix someone else and do it correctly?
We're here on earth to learn. Life is like a huge school. If we had
nothing to learn we probably wouldn't be here. Life gives us tremendous opportunities to learn things. It's easy to see the repercussions
of our actions. Matter is very convincing. It will come back and hit
us if we hit it. Add to that the fact that we get to communicate with
other people. We get immediate feedback, whether or not we choose
to see it. In the material world, life mirrors our beliefs and actions
right back at us. So, we learn how things work. More importantly, we
learn who we are and how we work. Some of us learn more quickly

ome lessons are more difficult, and others need to be
ın different ways.

ll have different lessons to learn and we all must learn
them differently. We have to find our own way. That's why we're
here. Each of us faces unique challenges and opportunities, all
requiring unique approaches. It isn't possible to fix someone else
correctly because we aren't that person. We're missing important
information that only that person has and there is no way for us to
fill in the blanks.

Even if we could fix someone, it would be better if we didn't.
Each person needs to find her own answers so she gets the lesson.
If we're trying to learn math we don't want someone else doing our
problems for us. We'd just have to find more problems to work so
that we could learn how to do them. If we fix someone's problem we
deprive the person of the opportunity of learning and growing. We
can support the person by giving requested resources or information. The best support of all is unconditional love and faith in the
person's ability to learn, to grow and to be successful. Our job is not

to fix others, but to learn our own lessons and respect each other's ability to learn and fix themselves.

The truth is, fixing others is not your job. If you think you have this job, fire yourself. If you are worried about someone, you're probably imagining how to go about fixing them. Instead of focusing on the process, turn your attention to the end result. Visualize him doing well – being happy and successful. Visualize love and compassion surrounding him. If someone asks you for advice you might say, "I can tell you what I'd do, but that may not work for you. However, I do know that you're capable, and I'm confident that you'll find your own answer. One that's right for you."

Now, what are you going to do with all of the time you've freed up by not trying to fix others?

Power Truth 7

Fixing others is not my job.

Limiting Belief 8

It has to make sense to be right.

T'ai Chi is a meditational, martial art – a powerful form of self-defense. It plays out like a very slow, meditative dance where the energy that is within and around you moves the body and spirit.

When I studied T'ai Chi I was told that moving slowly is more effective for teaching your body how to move quickly than moving fast. This slow dance form was practiced for thousands of years and yet its underlying principle made no sense to me. I practiced it on faith because it felt "right" to do it. Plus, I thought, "Who am I to argue with thousands of years of experience?" My mind argued that it was silly to learn how to move fast by going slowly. Still, I practiced T'ai Chi slowly, ignoring the impracticality of my actions. I never perfected the technique for moving quickly, or applying the actions in a defensive sequence.

One day I was walking down an alley and something fell behind me, making an astoundingly loud noise. Before I could think my body

speed, putting together postures in sequences

mastered. Instinctively, I felt poised and ready

My body moved faster than my mind and knew how

and itself without thinking. It had learned to move quickly by

going slow. It was true, even though the idea still didn't make sense.

A few years later I studied physiology in college. I learned that when we move slowly and repetitively the body builds up more synaptic fluid between the nerve junctions than when we move quickly. The body uses the synaptic fluid to transmit impulses from one nerve to the next. This fluid transmission is the slowest aspect of the nervous system. The more fluid we have, the faster the nerves transmit and the more quickly we move. T'ai Chi suddenly made perfect sense. It teaches us to move slowly so that we build up more synaptic fluid, among other things. It's fortunate that the Asian people didn't wait centuries to receive the full scientific explanation before practicing this very worthwhile art.

We're taught (incompletely) from childhood to only trust something if it makes sense. Yet that's only part of the equation.

Sometimes the truth doesn't make sense. It's also import
tune in to our feelings, along with our intuitive understanding a
insights. There is a lot to be gained from learning to also trust our
"gut" feelings and instincts.

I learned about vegetarianism in 1971. It felt right to me, so I
tried it. I first abstained from eating red meat and noticed that I felt
healthier. Then I eliminated poultry, fish and all seafood from my diet.
I felt lighter and more energized. It was the right diet for me, but it
made no sense to other people at the time. Friends literally told me
that I was crazy. A couple of physicians told me that I would die. They
were also worried about my daughter's diet when I became a mother.
I religiously paid attention to getting her the right amount of protein
and minerals. But I was told that she would become ill and weak. She
didn't. She was rarely ill, and now has one of the healthiest bodies
possible. Now many people are seeing the benefits of a vegetarian diet.
It's not right for everyone, but it's perfect for some. I'm glad I trusted
my inner knowing and how I felt. More than thirty years later I'm very
healthy, and know that my diet over the years had a lot to do with it.

to trust our intuition, even if we don't

's logic is critical to helping us function well.

practical knowledge isn't the only tool, and it isn't

right. Sometimes there are gaps in the information we need to process in order to come to the correct conclusions. Sometimes the truth defies logic. In order to live our best lives we need to trust all of our senses and balance them. Our feelings and intuition give us important insight that in many cases may be more accurate than logic.

The truth is, the truth doesn't always make sense. Sometimes you'll get a feeling that tells you to do something or say something and you won't understand why you should. Try trusting that feeling just once. Consciously do what your gut tells you to do. Or, what that voice in the back of your head speaks softly about. Write down your feelings at that moment and your decision based upon them. Then record the outcome in writing. You'll soon see that it makes sense to do what doesn't always make sense.

Power Truth 8

The truth doesn't always make sense.

Unlimited Life

Limiting Belief 9

I can consume whatever I want and it won't affect me.

There are a number of fuel options and most of us know which is the right one for getting the best performance from our cars. Even the most inexperienced driver knows that filling up the tank with molasses instead of gasoline will muck up the engine. We also know that living things run better on certain types of fuel. We feed our cats with the appropriate cat food. We water our plants with water and not orange juice. We even feed our babies well. We know that feeding newborn babies meat will cause indigestion. Yet, many of us assume that our bodies can magically live on foods that are not natural to it. We ingest chemicals and substances that we're not meant to handle, and believe that the body will process them without repercussions. We eat food that has little nutritional value and believe that our bodies will miraculously function at their peak. However, the reality is the body is an organic machine that acts in accordance to what it is fed. Give it low-grade fuel and it won't perform at its best. Feed it chemicals that it's not able to process and these chemicals will eventual cause it to break down. It's inevitable.

Two things contribute to the belief that our bodies can handle whatever we put into them. One, the body is absolutely amazing in its ability to recover. Break a leg, cut a finger, or develop a bruise from a fall and the body recovers remarkably. But, if we break a leg in the same place day after day it will stop healing well. In the same way, if we feed our body chemicals that cause an imbalance, it will eventually wear down. If we feed it too much sugar or fat our body will get sluggish. The brain is a part of the body. If it runs on the wrong fuel the thinking will be askew. The emotions will be off kilter. It's inevitable that this will happen.

We can put whatever fuel or poison in our bodies that we like. But, be aware that our bodies will function according to what we feed them. Your mind will reflect your diet. Your emotions will, as well. Your body is a living, breathing being that is capable of functioning very well if you just give it what it needs. If you feed it low-quality junk food it will struggle. If you learn to pay attention to what your body wants and feed it responsibly, you will find you're feeling better, thinking more clearly and you're happier.

The truth is that you reflect what you eat. You don't have to be a diet zealot. Sometimes you may want to give yourself an ice cream sundae. It's what you do most of the time that has the most effect. However, before you eat don't just focus on satisfying your craving or desire. Pay attention to your entire body. Imagine after eating the food how your body responds. If you pay close attention you will feel a subtle shift in your energy and how your body feels. Decide if you want to feel that way. The choice is yours.

Power Truth 9

My body, mind and spirit respond to what I eat.

Limiting Belief 10

I am my mind and/or body.

Who are you really? Most of us are trained to believe that we are the mind or body – the thing that has thoughts and feels sensations. We learn to identify with this part of ourselves and give ourselves a name.

Who are you when you wake up in the morning? Who are you before you think a thought and are merely aware that you're awake? Think about this. Now consider who is thinking about it.

There is a place of awareness within you that is the most important and powerful aspect of your self. It, more than any aspect of you, completely defines you as an entity. This part of you is separate from your mind and body. It is essentially aware and in touch with another level of information than the mind normally picks up.

As a nurse midwife I had the opportunity to observe and interact with babies immediately after they were born. Each baby has a unique presence that is apparent from the moment of birth. Each baby reacts differently to stimulus and other people according to its essential nature. I've seen babies scream and cry in reaction to the environment, as they take their first breath. Some babies are frightened, some angry, while others are merely calmly expressive. Some babies are peaceful when they're born. They look around and explore. The babies will often respond to their world in the same manner throughout their lives, unless trained to do otherwise.

As the babies slept, the nursing assistants and I would sometimes talk about them and what they would become in life. Even at one-day old, we knew them as individuals with characteristic natures. If you gaze into a baby's eyes, when he's not being distracted by the environment or his body you will come face-to-face with someone who is not thinking. He doesn't yet know his body and hasn't identified with it. He is merely an essential being, just being aware. You were this way, and a part of you still is.

Your body is not you. Neither is your mind or your emotions. Your mind, body and emotions are separate aspects of you in the physical. But you are more than the sum of these. Your inherent nature has an awareness that extends beyond the known physical. This aspect of self may seem profound and distant, but it is actually right here, right now. You are functioning from this place as you read this, though you may not be aware of it. You may have forgotten that baby person – forgotten who you really are.

Your life will change when you become aware of and focus on the essential nature that is attempting to guide you throughout your life. Your mind wants you to believe that you are it. It is an efficient machine-like aspect of the human body that wields great rational and technical powers. The mind, or brain, has the remarkable ability to manage large amounts of data and remember principles and ideas. It also has little faith in anything beyond itself and other minds. That is the nature of mind. It believes in itself as the powerful controller of the universe. It functions through understanding its own abilities and is strengthened through continued use. Like the muscles in your arms or legs, the more you use the mind, the more powerful it becomes. It is an effective tool, but it is not you.

You are an entity that watches and is aware of all that goes on around you. You are a being that is separate from the mind. When you realize this and identify with the essential being that you are, you are able to use the mind, instead of it using you. In a broader sense, you will have access to information and to a level of understanding that is not available to the mind.

When you recognize this essential point of awareness – the real you – you will be able to use all of your instincts and talents, and create from a place of new power and light.

If you find yourself worried, scattered, or confused. If you are caught up in your thoughts, or the feelings within your body. If you are engulfed in emotion, take a moment to notice. Notice who is noticing. Pay attention to this silent observer. Don't try to change your thoughts or emotions. Just notice them and be the being that's noticing. You can also do this when you're in a happy state. Pay attention to who you really are. With practice you will find that you are that observer more and more. You will then find a new sense of peace, fulfillment, and power – you will become aware. You will become the real you again.

Power Truth 10

I am not my body.
I am a unique, essential being living inside my body.

Unlimited Life

Limiting Belief 11

I'm on my own.

It's true. You are a unique entity with qualities that no one else shares. You are like an individual snowflake, amidst trillions of other snowflakes. You have your own vibration and essence that gives you a unique nature. You are special in this way and sometimes this uniqueness makes you feel alone. You may feel that no one completely understands you. But you are not alone.

Everything is energy. Including us. Humans and the other particles and beings on this planet are energy moving slowly – so slowly that the naked eye can see it. We call this slow moving energy "matter." We sometimes forget that we are just energy that is connected to other energy in one giant mass. Each burst of energy projects into the mass and moves the energy around it. Thoughts are energy. Feelings are energy. What we think and feel moves and effects the energy around us. Just as we are moved and affected by the energy around us.

One morning I awoke with a great sadness in me. I had no reason to feel sad. My life was going very well at the time. Yet, I felt so depressed. An hour later I turned on the news and saw that a tremendous earthquake had hit Turkey, and hundreds of thousands had been hurt or killed. I knew that I was picking up on the sadness of and for those people. Yes, I'm very sensitive and feel more than others, and this is an extreme example. However, you may also be affected more than you realize by the energy of others around you.

Have you ever had the experience of happily going about your day when someone angrily confronted you? Did you remain happy? Maybe you got angry back at him. Maybe you didn't feel angry towards the person, but felt anger within you. The energy was transmitted to you and through you and you reacted to that person.

How we react depends upon who we are and our present emotional and physical state. We feel each other's happiness, sadness, joy, and triumph... we move like molecules of water in the ocean. Each molecule is unique, but it is all a part of a greater entity that moves with the forces of the earth, the sky, the other molecules around it, and more. If you know and remember this you will never feel alone and disconnected.

The truth is you are always intricately connected. If you feel lonely or alone, or that you are not supported try doing the following: Sit quietly and stay centered within your body. Focus outside of you. Your molecules vibrate. Can you feel your skin vibrating? Visualize this vibration extending beyond your skin. Can you feel it? There is energy all around you. It is connected to all other energy. Everything you do affects everything around you, and visa verse. Perhaps you don't hear words or sounds, but the world is full of support for you. Breathe it in. Rejoice in it. Feel the grace that surrounds you and let yourself bask in it.

Power Truth 11

I am unique and intricately connected to all and everything.

Limiting Belief 12

My worth is determined by what I do.

You are a unique entity. Your essence radiates like the sun in your world. Your energy affects everything around you. You affect the world just by being you. No one can contribute what you can. You, just sitting and being you affects and contributes to the world around you.

It's natural for us to want to be productive. This drive stems from our human survival instinct. We naturally delight in seeing the effects of our efforts and creativity on the world. It's the reason why babies delight in their own bowel movements; and why older children love to see how their body affects finger paints on paper, or mud. We spend hours building sand castles that get washed away. We create new technologies and build rocket ships as well as new and improved washing machines. We raise children, cure diseases and run banks. What we do is a reflection of who we are. And, being unique, we each have something different to contribute to society. Wanting to DO something with our lives is both natural and healthy.

Sometimes we get hung up on this need to DO something and we forget about who we are being. We feel like failures if we don't accomplish something that is seen as worthwhile in our eyes or the eyes of others. This frustration and feeling of failure brings us down in spirit and causes our vibration to weaken. Our "being-ness" is devalued.

Life is meant to be an adventure. Whatever we do with our life is part of this adventure. As individual entities we are free to choose whatever adventure we want to have. Our choices of what we do in the adventure are appropriate, as long as we don't intentionally hurt another or ourselves. No adventure is better than another. The journey will be more pleasant if we choose something that suits our essential nature. This path is often referred to as "following your heart." Sometimes we trip up and other times we build. Sometimes we lead nations and other times we raise hamsters. If we do what we love we blossom, no matter the end result. Still, we don't have to do anything to be worthwhile. Each one of us adds to the universe just by being here.

I met a woman at a luncheon who had recently moved to another town in order to be with her new husband. In doing so she had to give up her job. This woman was lovely, intelligent and vibrant. I felt an instant connection that made me want to get to know her better.

The woman volunteered that had she been very successful in her career and had achieved financial independence. You would think she took pride in the fact that she he didn't have to work. But, instead of rejoicing in her situation she felt restless and incomplete. She said, "I judge who I am by what I do. I don't feel as if I am a successful as a person if I'm not successful in a career." She firmly believed in this and there was no room for her to see that her entire being wasn't framed by what she did for a living. She couldn't see what I saw – this lovely, warm and vibrant being. Many people share the same belief. Some achieve success and realize that it is not a measure of worth. If they don't know who they are they may become depressed and despondent.

Creation is a great joy. Success can be a lot of fun. But, you are not what you succeed at. You are so much more.

Power Truth 12

No matter what I do, I contribute to the world by being here.

Limiting Belief 13

Happiness is merely a state of mind or emotion.

As we know, being happy is not something that's achieved through circumstances. We can hang out in the best environment, with fascinating people, enjoying perfect weather... and still feel miserable. Why? Happiness can't be earned and it isn't created externally. It's an energy that we choose to embody or not.

Recently my husband Dave and I were talking about the importance of happiness in our lives. We truly are happy in every sense of the word, and yet we still have bad or grumpy days. I wasn't feeling that I had the right to be grumpy. I thought that regardless of whether my life was satisfying, or not I "should" be happy all of the time. Yet, I noticed that I was having periods when I felt just middle of the road happy, and sort of blah. I wasn't happy about that.

I was feeling compassion for friends and others around me that have experienced some terrible tragedies and faced difficult situations.

This made me even more grateful for my life. I had absolutely no reason to complain and yet I was feeling like a failure because I was not all together happy. This self-criticism was fueling my waves of unhappiness. Beating myself up always works to bring me down. I wanted out. I'd had enough and I was ready to get happy again.

First, I gave myself permission to be unhappy. I told myself that I didn't need a reason; I could dwell in misery as long as I liked, it was my choice. So there! I needed to stop beating me up and just let myself mope if that's what was on the agenda for the day.

That exercise was enough to free me of the need to be unhappy. Next, I chose to bring in happiness. Dave and I imagined gold suns above our heads. We filled these suns with happy and joyful energy. When we allowed the suns to open up and shower us with this energy voila! We were filled with being happy. Nothing changed externally, but it worked.

Lately I've been exploring the state of being unhappy and came to the conclusion that "unhappiness" is a term that's overused. When we allow ourselves to become drained of energy – all energy – we call this the state of being "unhappy." This low-down feeling can also be expressed as "unlove," "ungrace," "unpower," and "unenergized." We can fill this void with happiness, if we choose. We can also fill up with love, grace, power, or any positive vibration, and experience the feeling of fullness and happiness. All it takes is visualizing a sun. Or, imagine taping into the energy that you want to bring in and simply filling yourself up with it.

Given this self-healing option, why do we sometimes choose to continue feeling depleted? Often its because we feel overwhelmed by circumstances and by other people. One of the ways we choose to react to this state of affairs is to go into a "cave" and withdraw. We decide, or create an intention that new information will come in and take the pressure off if we go low enough. It does. I've tried it. I've gotten more and more depressed and withdrawn. When the proverbial "empty tank" light went on in me I immediately began to fill back up. It was like exhaling to empty and inhaling to fill right back up. Information and understanding, love or joy filled the void. Perhaps you have this intention at times. Is it the best way to get over your state of energetic depletion?

Do we have to exhale completely in order to draw in new information? Do we create this struggle with the light and dark – fullness and emptiness – in order to experience drama in our lives? Many things run in cycles: A symphony will most likely contain arias that are very quiet and peaceful, where the notes almost stand still. Then the cymbals or brass section fires up and we are filled with a cacophony of musical sound. Exhale and inhale. Is it essential? We know it creates excitement, but do we have to suffer in order to grow and learn?

Experience has shown me that life is a series of challenges. Sometimes we let ourselves become drained by them. Or, we may become drained of energy by others. In any case, we allow ourselves to be depleted of energy and fuel. When this happens we can become mired in that unhappy place. Do we have a "right" to be unhappy? We certainly do. We can go into a cave and hold onto depletion. Or, we can decide to fill up.

Unhappiness can strike anywhere, as it did when I was having lunch one day at a neighborhood restaurant and the server treated me very rudely. My blood started to boil as the irritation built up inside of me. But I stayed aware of what was happening within me and thought, "I'm having a great day. Do I want to let this person spoil it for me?" I decided right then and there that I could choose to let this incident bother me or I could choose happiness. I chose happiness. I let the irritation go and decided instead to be happy. I also took the opportunity to inform the manager, because I believe in always supporting good customer service.

Happiness is a vibration. It's energy. Happy isn't something we create. We can't buy it and we can't earn it. Everyone has the right to it. We choose it in every moment. We have the right to be depleted. We also have the right to be happy, no matter the circumstances.

Meditation is a powerful tool for filling up with happiness – or just plain filling up. You can begin by sitting quietly and paying attention to the state of your energy level. If your energetic fuel tank is low, work on filling it up. You may ask yourself where and when are you getting drained? You can then visualize plugging this hole in your life by deciding that you will be filled with light.

When you're sad, realize that you are choosing to be that way. You can choose to stay that way. Or, you can consciously decide that you want to be happy. It's as simple as it seems if you believe it. The choice is yours.

Power Truth 13

Happy is a form of energy and having it is a choice we make.

Limiting Belief 14

I need to avoid making mistakes.

I experienced a remarkable revelation while skiing one winter with my sister. We were traversing down a slope and I inadvertently crossed the front tips of my skis. Even non-skiers can see that this will cause some problems. Usually it leads to me falling straight forward – if not on my face, then on some part of my upper body. I've been trying for years to correct this inconvenient lapse in proper skiing form, but obviously without enjoying much success. However, this time I instantly lifted my top ski, steadied myself and corrected my mistake – all while going downhill at a pretty fast pace. I felt irritated with myself that I'd "done it again." I'd crossed my ski tips. Then it occurred to me that this time I didn't fall. I wasn't on the ground cursing and brushing the snow off of my face and glasses. I recovered from my mistake. I'd learned how to correct and continue on, and I'd done it effortlessly.

Watching the Olympics I've often seen competitive skiers almost fall. Usually the athlete corrects her error and sometimes wins the race. At the end of the day, the athletes standing on the winner's stand aren't necessarily the most careful skiers and their form isn't always perfect. But they outperform the others by pushing themselves beyond their previous limitations. Sure, they make mistakes. But they're able to correct themselves, maintain their balance and move on. They win because they constantly push themselves beyond the limits of their ability. They learn and grow. Great skiers fall, get up and fall numerous times more before they learn how to adjust and ski better.

It occurred to me that because I had learned from my mistakes on the slopes I was less likely to repeat them and wind up on my face in the snow again. OK, so I wasn't an Olympic champion and I wasn't flying through slalom gates. But, learning this was very important to me. It meant that I was skiing and not lying on the mountain. I felt pretty impressed with myself that I'd learned how to correct my mistake.

A few years later, I was working out with my fitness trainer, Joseph, and he had me doing a particularly difficult exercise. I was holding a free weight in my right hand and balancing myself on my left leg. He then had me bend down and touch the weight in front of my left leg, while keeping the right leg raised. At the same time I was balancing an expensive China dinner plate in my mouth... (O.K. I lied about the plate).

To complicate matters, I was standing on a foam pad at the time, so my left foot was not on solid ground. It took a number of tries before I was able to do this without dropping my right leg, or grabbing onto Joseph's arm for support. I was eventually able to accomplish it, but my left foot and ankle constantly shifted and wobbled to maintain the balance. It didn't look pretty, but, I did it. My leg and body learned how to accomplish the exercise utilizing the newly strengthened muscles in my foot, ankle and knee to stabilize me. I was pushing my limits and I was growing.

Noted scientist Thomas J. Watson said, "The way to succeed is to double your error rate." If we were able to accomplish every goal on the very first try, there would be nothing new, or challenging in life. A growth filled life is laden with errors. If we don't constantly try and fail and try again, we are staying within the safety net of our previous experience. Instead of offering new adventures, each day would be exactly like the day before. When we push our limits we sometimes wobble and fall, but eventually we learn. We are then stronger, wiser and in a sense bigger than before. Thomas Edison invented the light bulb on his ten thousandth try. That's 9,999 mistakes. If we're not making mistakes, we're missing opportunities to grow and expand. Honor and applaud your mistakes.

One way to appreciate our mistakes is to laugh at them lovingly. I was standing in the kitchen next to a dear, aging friend. His physical condition had deteriorated terribly, and he didn't have complete control of his bodily functions. He began to walk towards the sink and as did he let out a very long and loud fart. I didn't know what to do or say. It was an awkward situation, yet it was too obvious to ignore. He made it easy for me though. He turned, facing me with a half-laughing grin on his face and said, "I didn't really want to walk over here. The gas propelled me." We both started to laugh hysterically. I laughed until I had tears in my eyes. It was a wonderful moment that I'll never forget. He loved and trusted in himself enough to enjoy himself, even when he made an embarrassing mistake.

Try laughing at yourself joyously once in awhile. You may find that you're better able to appreciate yourself and your mistakes.

Power Truth 14

Mistakes are laurels on our way to mastery of the new.

Unlimited Life

Limiting Belief 15

I'm wasting my time when I'm idle.

An elderly friend who was raised on a farm often spoke about his experiences as a child. He shared insights that held great meaning for me: "I was a child in a time when there was nothing to do but make a living. We had to slave in the fields and make our lives more profitable by working from day through night. But, it was not thought of as work. It was just what we did. We didn't think about going to work in the fields. We thought about planting the corn. We thought about cutting the peas. We watered crops and took care of the cattle. Yet we still had time between activities to sit around and watch the animals as they grazed. Though we didn't think of one as an activity and the other as non-activity. We just had time."

"There was no concept of wasting time when I was growing up," he said. "There was going hungry because the corn wasn't planted. There were times when the cows would moo because they needed milking. Things just happened and you did what was there to do when it was time."

"When there was nothing to do, nothing was done," he continued. "Nothing was really something, because there's actually a lot going on when you don't have a chore to focus on. There were birds in the sky. There was shifting in the weather to take note of. There were pages of paper to write on, paints to draw with and thoughts to focus on. These were very precious times – when the mind could wander and say what it had learned."

"Contemplation makes the world go round," he said. "It's when the creative inspiration and message happens. It's when the looks of love between a parent and child occur. It's those silent spaces between tasks that are full of life. If we slept, we needed rest. There was no justifying a nap. It just happened."

Somewhere along the line certain tasks and the time it takes to do them have been labeled as "quality time." Other times are not. There's a sense that the times when we're not actively engaged in doing something are less valuable, or meaningful. But, just the opposite is true: They're invaluable. Idle time is when we fill up with all we've done.

Everything we do or don't do contributes to our experience. So, no matter what we're doing we're experiencing. If we loaf and don't do our chores, for example, we get hungry and we learn from it. If we are overworked and don't take the time to contemplate and rest, we get angry and frustrated. We lose our peace and joy. We experience in a different way and we still learn.

No matter how the time is spent, it's important to be aware – to be present. When we're acting blindly – 'asleep at the wheel', so to speak – we are not present. This can happen when we're mindlessly working on a repetitive task, or just spacing out. In either case our time is not wasted. Time continues on with us, or without us. When we are not present time is not wasted, but rather, its a waste of us. When we're present we're absorbing whatever happens. We're experiencing. We're learning and evolving. No matter what we do.

There is a tendency to feel a sense of guilt when we're not actively engaged, or doing something positive. This is a misdirected feeling of obligation. It results in a loss of appreciation and value of all that is going on and happening around us. It's important to appreciate the pauses – the "down time" – and see that every moment is equally valuable when we're present and aware.

Power Truth 15

No matter what I do, my time is worthwhile if I am aware.

Limiting Belief 16

I need to have an opinion – to take a side.

It is part of human nature to judge the world around us. As mammals, we're constantly scanning our environment and the other people and beings in it, in order to feel safe and secure. We use critical analysis to judge whether or not we are functioning appropriately in different situations. This way of sizing up the world is genetically programmed and aligned, and it works like a machine. We make judgements based on the data accumulated in past generations and by our own past impressions. We use this form of judgment to orient ourselves in the world.

The body is an excellent judge of the world around it. It has been genetically programmed to accept many forms of information that we may not be conscious of in other ways. The body knows how to orient itself within space and time. It knows to recognize dangers around it in order to protect itself. The mind will often interpret these signals and create judgments about them. For instance, through-out the centuries different races have been at war. Genetically and energetically the combatants were programmed to dislike and fear each other. To this day, the same basic programming is carried forward. Their descendents may notice these same signals of fear, rage and distrust when they meet.

People also display programming picked up during this life-time. We may have had an experience that created an impression that still influences us. For example, as a child a dog may have attacked us, and now we inherently suspect that all dogs will harm us. As an aware being, we can reprogram these thoughts, or discount them, knowing now that not all dogs are vicious.

We are also programmed when people around pass judgment on others. These judgments are accepted at face value, passed on, and programmed into us if we allow it. For example, if a mother tells her daughter that wearing a short dress is immoral, she might see others who are dressed this way as being immoral. Consequently, the daugh-ter avoids revealing clothes. This judgment does not necessarily serve the daughter. She may like these fashions and be able to wear them appropriately, but she won't wear them now because of this judgment. She may also wrongly interpret the morals of other women wearing revealing clothes.

It is possible to energetically reprogram the information we receive genetically and environmentally. We can easily reprogram ourselves by staying neutral.

There are three perspectives in life: Positive, negative and neutral. There is a "yes" for every "no," a "near" to every "far," and a neutral counterpoint to every negative or positive aspect in life. When we identify strongly with one side of the perspective we miss the information coming from the other side. If we remain positive all of the time we miss important negative information. If we remain negative we miss the positive point of view. There is a way to receive all information and determine it it's appropriate for us. Take a third stance – one that's neutral. If we take a stance then consciously step back and identify with neither side – we will be in a third place of neutrality.

This place of neutrality is what is referred to as an objective viewpoint. Since we are not vouching for any particular side, we're able to see all sides accurately. For example, we can objectively observe a debate on the effects of a vegetarian diet on the body. Some people will tell us that it is harmful to the body. Others will say that it's healthier. If we remain neutral and avoid supporting either side of the argument, we can hear both sides with an open mind. Then we can decide which side makes the most persuasive case and compare it with your own experience. Do we feel healthier when we eliminate animal products from our diet? Perhaps we can see the truth in the arguments of others and come up with our own evaluation based upon a neutral stance. Being neutral does not mean being noncommittal. If we remain neutral, we're able to change our ideas as the circumstances change and not be tied to one view or the other.

When we look at the world around us we see points of reference that are aligned with one side of reality or another. We see people yelling at each other, and that may represent negative behavior to us. Or we see people hugging each other, and that may seem positive.

When we label these behaviors for better or for worse, we're judging them. We're taking a stance about which behavior is appropriate, or positive, and which is not.

However, all may not be what it seems and it might help to dig a little deeper. Perhaps the people arguing actually love each other. Maybe they see yelling as a means of expressing themselves. This is the way they not only communicate their feelings, but also learn to understand each other better. In such a case the interaction may seem negative, but it is the way these people choose to communicate and it works for them.

Similarly, the openly affectionate couple we observe strolling through the park may be committing adultery – which could negatively impact their lives and the lives of their families. Or, maybe they're affectionate out of obligation and actually hate each other. In that case they're being untrue to themselves.

My parents argue. They always have. That may seem like an insurmountable problem, but they've been arguing and happily married for fifty-eight years. Something's obviously working for them.

It takes an amalgam of negative, positive and neutral forces for the universe to function normally. This is readily apparent when we examine atomic particles. An atom needs three aspects: a neutrino (neutral), a positron (positive), and an electron (negative). Without these elements the atom doesn't exist. All three forces are necessary in the basic composition of the world.

Each year wildfires tear apart the landscape of forests. Many trees are killed and plant life is destroyed. This is necessary for rich soil to form and for new growth to occur. The burned out areas sprout smaller plants, which feed the wildlife and regenerate the soil. While these events are occurring, the sun rises and sets; everything else is essential to the process while remaining neutral to it.

To see things from a neutral perspective it's best to note not only the positive and negative, but also consider everything else. For example: A father and daughter might argue about whether or not the daughter may go out on a date. There are negative and positive sides leading to opposite conclusions: "Yes, I can," and "No, you can't."

This argument could continue for hours, days, and even years.

However, there are many other alternatives because everything else still exists outside of this argument. At the exact same moment a salesperson is calling on a restaurant in Florence, Italy. There are people talking outside the house. A car accident is occurring in Australia. None of this seems relevant to the argument. But, nothing in life (including communication and thought) can occur without the influence of everything else around it. If the father and daughter let go of the "yes and no" of the situation and remain objective – remain aware that everything else is happening – another solution might occur. A party invitation might appear creating an opportunity for the daughter to go with the date, but also be with others. Or perhaps the couple might go to a school sponsored event where the parents are also in attendance. There are many alternatives to all situations. It's impossible to be open to them when you've identified with the positive or negative side of either interaction or question.

Negative, positive and neutral energies affect us when we're trying to make a decision. The V.P. of procurement at a company may be wondering if he should buy a certain product. He'd been told about the product and is considering it, but isn't sure if it's right for the company's needs. Will it cost too much? Will it save him money? Will the C.E.O. approve? The key to solving a dilemma like this is to step back from the situation and focus on anything not related to it. He can remove himself from the outcome and look at the situation objectively. Perhaps there's another solution beyond this one. Doing more research might help firm up his decision.

One way effective salespeople create a neutral environment for their clients is to meet them on the golf course without the pressure of impending business decisions. In this neutral space, decisions are subtly made without having to hash out the "yes" and "no" of an idea. As we are able to step back and see all perspectives, decisions will come to us naturally from a place of neutrality. Once we've got the total picture we can act accordingly.

When you find yourself locked in a debate or unable to make a decision, step back and identify with a more neutral aspect of reality. Remove your awareness from the outcome and center yourself. Let go of the result and become aware of the rest of the world. Listen to a bird singing, or notice the sun rays reflecting on a car. DO, or THINK anything that is unrelated to the issue at hand. Notice the shift in energy and then pursue your activity from this perspective. You'll notice that your body relaxes more, your mind is freed up to evaluate more accurately, and you'll be feeling happier and more content.

A neutral stance is also essential when we're helping others. Let's say that you're talking to someone who is unhappy. If you identify with the positive or negative aspect of the conversation, you'll get bogged down and become enmeshed with the other person's energy. Suppose you are a close friend of a woman that loses her husband to cancer. This is a very sad situation. She may be crying and telling you how lonely and distraught she is. If you allow yourself to identify with her, and become like her, you too will become lonely and distraught. Then you'll both be stuck in the same place. There is no hope of seeing the light when you're both wallowing in this negative space.

The other alternative is to remain neutral. I'm not saying to stop having any feeling for the woman. You can feel a great deal of compassion or love for her, which is not as obvious to her when you're lonely and unhappy like her. If you compassionately listen from a place of neutrality — without taking on her negative energy — you will become a beacon of positive thinking and hope. She can connect with this place within you that is not sinking into despair. This will be a lifeboat that she can focus on consciously or unconsciously, and eventually her sadness may give way to peace.

In the same way, a good salesperson can lose a sale by being too positive about a product. Trying too hard to show the product in a positive light (identifying with the positive energy) might create the opposite effect; the client could feel overwhelmed and back away. By remaining objective, the salesperson can talk to the client about what she needs. The salesperson can talk about other things, as well. She can tell the client about the product from a neutral space, stressing its positive aspects, but not identifying with the outcome. If she takes herself out of the equation, she'll give the client the space to make the decision on her own terms. From a space of neutrality, the salesperson will be able to observe what the client really needs. She'll be able to ask questions that help her to understand the client's motivations and concerns. If the salesperson can provide useful information, and if the timing is right and the product is beneficial to her, the client will most likely buy the product.

When we exist in a place of neutrality, we're able to see all of life in a relaxed and easy manner. We won't get caught up in the outcome of events. We'll exist in a place of awareness where we know that everything is moving as it should, and that everything will unfold in time. We'll feel secure because we won't be attached to a particular outcome. Our happiness will not depend upon events and how they play out. Instead we will exist in a place of pure bliss, which knows only present time. It is from this place that we'll be able to create great miracles in our life.

The truth is, we make better decisions when we act from a place of neutrality. Remind yourself of this when you are angry or arguing. Are you stuck in a dichotomy? Realize that you are stuck and are not getting the big picture. To get unglued try thinking of something totally unrelated. For example, say you're debating with your spouse. She says that the two of you need to go on a vacation. You say that the two of you should save your money instead. Back and forth it goes. There seems like there's no way out.

Take a break for awhile and let the issue sit. Try changing the subject. Or try talking about anything else. How's your mother doing? Did the dog get fed? Did you enjoy your workout today? Then, let go of your place on the dichotomy. You'll find that you'll gain a new perspective on the situation that can serve as a catalyst for exploring totally new solutions.

Power Truth 16

*By staying neutral I see all aspects
of reality and make appropriate choices.*

Unlimited Life

Conclusion

Through the proceeding chapters we've explored how common limiting beliefs may be standing in the way of our happiness; and preventing us from having the life we dreamed of. Replacing these beliefs with powerful truths is the first step towards unblocking ourself so that we can avoid many of the stressful times of our life.

We can all learn a lesson from the University of Georgia Basketball team. UGA posted the worst record of any SE Conference basketball team in 2007, winning only four conference games all season. Nobody gave them a chance in the SEC Championship Tournament at the end of the year. Nobody thought of them as winners. There was even talk that the coach would be fired. But UGA overcame all odds and won four straight games over a weekend tournament (two games played and won in the same day due to a change in venue caused by a tornado that damaged the Georgia Dome) to win the SEC Championship and a berth in the NCAA tournament.

So, despite seemingly impossible odds, they won as many conference games in a single weekend as they had won all year.

University of Florida coach Billy Donovan was quoted in the Atlanta Journal, as saying, "You're talking about one of the most incredible stories in college basketball this season, maybe the best. It's a great lesson for people in life that, if there's perseverance, if there's a passion, if there's an intensity and enthusiasm and a belief in what you're doing, things can happen like that."

Always remember, you are the master creator of your life – you define your life according to what you believe. Your beliefs are a part of you and your life is shaped around them. Your thoughts and beliefs define YOU. Are you stuck? Are you stressed or unhappy? Do you feel like you aren't moving as effectively as you could? It may be that some of your beliefs do not serve you. Try letting go of these beliefs and replace them with truths or other beliefs that work for you.

Your beliefs can trip you up, or they can set you free. You can choose what you believe. Choose wisely.

16 Power Truths

1. If I'm asked to do something, I'm capable of doing it.

2. Time is unlimited. I have as much time as I need.

3. Projects will take as much time as I intend them to.

4. I can create anything I dream, one step at a time.

5. When Life changes, I change. I learn and move forward.

6. You can see eye-to-eye, but you can't walk in another's shoes.

7. Fixing others is not my job.

8. The truth doesn't always make sense.

9. My body, mind and spirit respond to what I eat.

10. I am not my body. I am a unique, essential being living inside my body.

11. I am unique and infinitely connected with all and everything.

12. No matter what I do, I contribute to the world by being here.

13. Happy is a form of energy and having it is a choice we make.

14. Mistakes are laurels on our way to mastery of the new.

15. No matter what I do, my time is worthwhile if I am aware.

16. By staying neutral I see all aspects of reality and make appropriate choices.

About Deborah Hill

Deborah Hill is actively helping others to transform their lives and situations as an Intuitive Coach, Counselor, Speaker and Teacher. She has practiced healing and counseling throughout her adult life; first as a Registered Nurse and Nurse-Midwife, and finally as an intuitive coach and counselor, energetic therapist and artist. Her life experiences include degrees in natural resources, nursing and psychology, 18 years as an entrepreneur running her own business, and raising her wonderful daughter. Deborah has extensively studied many forms of natural and traditional healing, as well as counseling, coaching and spiritual disciplines with several teachers throughout her life. She now lives in Atlanta, Georgia and Greensboro, North Carolina with her husband.

For more information, please contact
Malaya Creations
5269 Glenridge Drive, Atlanta, GA 30342
877-462-5292

www.YourIntuitiveLife.com

Made in the USA